Scarlet Clock

Scarlet Clock

Kilayla Pilon

RESOURCE *Publications* · Eugene, Oregon

SCARLET CLOCK

Resource Publications
An Imprint of Wipf and Stock Publishers
199 W. 8th Ave., Suite 3
Eugene, OR 97401

www.wipfandstock.com

PAPERBACK ISBN: 978-1-6667-3785-1
HARDCOVER ISBN: 978-1-6667-9786-2
EBOOK ISBN: 978-1-6667-9787-9

FEBRUARY 15, 2022 2:25 PM

THE CLOCK TICKS as the dial turns
The thrumming hum of clicking gears the only sound
For silence is all that echoes inside that home
Save for the chime of another hour passed
Each moment a tempo beating through
As if ripping wounds in place
To those who hear the pendulum swing, to hear the gears grinding
They are reminded of the sorrow each new day can bring
As it marks one more second, minute, hour
Where the love that once sat laughing at the creaking dining room table
Decorated in Christmas holiday cloth and candles
Plates piled high and echoing grins as clinking cutlery filled the air
Sit now in silence with dusty fallen fair
Love lingers in the scrambled, torn paper sheets
Just as known that she is no longer here
The clock ticks as the dial turns

WHAT MUST IT be to feel that strange, foreign emotion
I tremble at its name, the fear flows through my veins
It has spread across my skin, starting from my beating heart
As the crimson spills in overflow and the delicate layers
They have split apart, in pieces of shredded misery
This emotion is one that many seek
Some climb mountains as tall as Everest
In search of something more, something worth dying for
I suppose I can relate to that
The risk of death for something more, something less that pales
A comparison chart would do no good
A fleeting glimpse into the eyes of those who know
That love is the emotion I seek
With risk and determination I must climb to the highest peak
Risking death in the cold, pressurized air
Just to feel as if I belong somewhere

It was a darkness of her mind
A feeling she couldn't escape
So she dug a grave, every day
Built of marrow and decay
But she worked with endless effort
To find a place of beauty
In the corpses of her emotions
As she lay them in their wedded bliss
With deaths final ending kiss
A rain that poured from nowhere
The droplets bled on her skin
For the sorrow she felt grew
With every lightning flash that cracked
Ripping open the sky
She knew that her dark and battered soul
Would wage war with no end in sight
Just as she knew the droplets of rain
Had stained her once again
With thin red lines of a pain sublime

CURIOSITY POSED a question of the sound
A sound only heard once or twice for some, when true pain came with a
bloody slice
Would it ring out like a crying widow at night?
Would it clash like cymbals and cause a fright?
Yet honesty found many would be surprised
To discover the chaos that echoed and lingered in wait
Had formed deep within her soul, so dark, so tainted
And the pain only served to speak the words of chaos
In the sight of blood droplets on a toilet paper roll

How WOULD ONE describe it
The sorrow that ate its way through her soul
Tied puppet strings to her fragile, broken limbs
It was not without a fight
For she caused much trife
But the sorrow, it did win
When she bled at its hands
Once again

Is IT A DARKNESS in my soul, my love?

That breeds a pain

No one has ever known?

Yet how cruel to assume that my pain was brand new

For the hurt within me was not something I dared spill from my lips like a journalist at his keys

I could not understand how others stood like stone with swords at the ready

Their minds strong and their hearts filled

Despite the blood stained trails that lived in the past

While I lay on the floor, bleeding heavy with every breath a choking gasp

I suppose the darkness that spilled from every gaping wound,

May as well have been an escaping segment of my defeated, sorrowful soul

OH SUCH SORROW, such common misery
When I pressed hot metal into my chest
Burned away the scars left on my breast
From hands that had left the bruise
Upon my pounding and shivering heart
It was me who liked to be a masterpiece
Perhaps a work of fragile art,
So every scar that split my skin
Made me realize I was instead alarming
No longer a beauty, no longer free
For his hands had enveloped me
Showing up on my skin in pink tyranny

I KEEP MY LIPS pressed in a thin line
Words I want to say refusing to pass my by in a gentle whisper
As if the moment my lips part
A wave of blood will spill from my heart
I forget what I'm talking about in the middle of a sentence
I've forgotten the color of my own mother's eyes
Pondering questions of a reality, of what it means to feel joy that doesn't
come from a drug
Or to not feel angry waiting to hear back from a plug
I'm geared on a path of destruction
Anticipating my total annihilation
My wheels won't turn without that first bump, they're locked in position
Soon enough spinning with the new fuel and the keys in the ignition
Like the blood from my mouth that covers the track, the wheels screech
stripes of black
Racing down to the end of this slip and slide road
Where there is nothing to see but stains of my reality
And some part of me does nothing, not a single attempt to stay safe
Because God, what a rush, to tempt fate

WHEN THE SUN broke free from dark scenery
While words so sweetly tumbled
From the mouth of the unloving
It was pain that I had wrought
Listening to his voice as if decaying rot
I had to wonder if it was selfish to hope and dream, to daydream freely
Of the day he lay six feet beneath me
And the final scar that he had left
Was no longer screaming tragedy
But instead a reminder of brevity
That I had tossed aside from my own longevity

I REMEMBER THOSE days
As my forlorn heart sailed
Upon a crashing sea of navy waves
Where dark skies loomed with rumbling clouds of rage consumed
Yet I braved the tides that tossed me with fury
In hopes that one day, when my boat came to reach the shore
The distance that separated us would be closed forever more

Was it love or was it pain that had done it to me?

Taken me to a dark place of deprivation

Where I had dug into my skin with not a thought to the ungodly sin

Felt the shred of a vein and the crimson that smelled like tin

It made me wonder how much it would cost to sew

The wounded parts within my heart that felt so conflicted yet lead to such macabre art

I HAD TO wonder if I was weak
Or perhaps if I had just gone one day too long
Without a new laugh to wander through the air
Like the musical notes of that one rock fair
Too long since your eyes once saw me laugh
A laugh I cannot see for myself, for the mirror ages me twenty years
Nor can my heart cope with the idea of being held in the arms of anybody
else, because no one will have the softness of you
No one held such beauty, such soulful grace
It would be an act of rebellion to fall for someone who could bring such a
smile to my otherwise somber expression

I MISS EACH DAY when you hummingbird heart would be beating against my chest

Now replaced by the empty rumbling of the air conditioner

And so I lay alone in a blanket, one made soft and heavy

A blanket that I toss and turn beneath

Pulling close to my skin, hoping for just that hummingbird moment

When I would feel as if I held you

As if to pretend the warmth pressing against me

Was any comparison to the last moment

I saw you

Beneath the warmth of home
One I have never known quite as well
Since the days that had come
When your arms held me in a warm embrace
Your breath tickling my skin as we laughed
The feel of your head rested against my thumping chest
When your eyes as soft as a sunrise sky eyes held mine
That day, that life was I nothing could compare to since you had left
And so I lay with a few days left
Beneath the blankets where I have wept
Of the cruel reality
That is the absence of you
Creating an absence
Of me

DEEP SCREAMING AGONY, for sorrows just not the same
As a blade and forty ounces keep calling in vain
She could see the grass on the other side of the window
The blooming flowers as spring settled in
The soft blue sky where plumes of gentle white clouds hovered
She felt the chains dig into her skin as she dared even contemplate
Invisible were the chains, though she imagined them to be dark and
rusted with age
Blood splatters long dried against the metal shine in her visualization
Reminders of her attempts to break free of the confinement caused by he
Whose hands had dragged across her skin
She preferred the chains stinging bite

Weight bearing memories fell as the bricks of her walls came crumbling
Pain crushing and tight like the dull ache in her skull
Every inch of her unbathed skin
Confined kept in the darkness she so longed to escape
Some had come in gentle words
A reminder of a world with songbirds
She had reminded of the scars as the chains tugged
They told her the chains were not there, that she was free
They did not understand nor could they see
No matter the mightiest swing to break the rusted metal
Save for a small chip or a small dent put in place
The chains had become a part of her

I WILL FOREVER be a participant in tragedy
Through a life blended into misery
But still I breathe and still I fight
For every breath escaping me
Brings me closer to my yearned for reality
While I may sit on a throne of sorrow
I know there will always be a tomorrow

Childhood freedom believing the tales
Dancing princesses with cascading hair
Twinkling lights of fairy delight
A swan, wings poised to take flight
What it must be like
For youthful hope to blossom
Instead the story speaking
Blood spilled into magenta pools
Silver glints, razor blades
Gentle were the tales, judgemental were the eyes
Desperation at its best
It would not have been a fairy tale
Without the failure, without the jest
Shadowed remnants had come to play
Tearing apart the stories, the worlds, the games
That once seemed to be so magically far away
Now alone, now in the water
She bled red, a single question posed
Childhood freedom, childhood homes -
How many had she been forced to know
Before she'd discovered the truth, the pinnacle point
That a tale is a story, a grand imagination
In similar ways that the girl remembered
Divine intervention as she sunk
Deeper into the crimson waters
For her freedom no longer came
From witches who cackled with cats on their brooms
Or ogres and donkeys so different in feud
But in the way she could split her pale soul
Into shattered, fractured pieces
Of her own fairy tale

WATER OF CRYSTAL clear creativity is always a work of art
In those who use the gentle acts, where scrubbing paint and primer stains
Is being born anew with a fresh idea bubbling through
Yet for me it was much more blue
For the water did run red and spilled over the sides of the sink
Dripping, dripping and staining the linoleum floor
I wished my water had never shown me
Such a masochist reality

HALLWAYS THAT TWIST and wind so fascinate me
Yet the winding path that I have traveled
Was one of blue lines and signs that spoke
Of emergency rooms, acute care
Intensive care and bedside alarms as i waited once again
Because I had given in to the haunting reality That my veins are just as
fascinating
Or so it says, in memory

I HAVE NO MORE words to speak

No fancy lies of twisted divine intervention

Unless one should count the deep screams echoing into an abyss that taunts me

With the depth I'd fall, my wings no longer catching the mismatched razor blades that shred my skin

Courage is what it would take to take that step

Final freedom and the fearful excitement burns in my crimson stained chest

Abysmally drained, exhaustion keeping the actions at bay despite the chanting words

It lingers in my poisoned mind, that endless thought

Unanswered prose of burning crows as they scream into the night

The thoughts as they echo and strike fearful horror

Dare I venture to crawl from this bed in which I lay

Where the sheets provide a world of peace

A gentle silence, a poetic lease as it keeps me contained in the shadows of my cloaked bedroom

Or shall I never have to move again, with my finally breath choking on bloodstained lines of poetry that never leave my fragile mind

Still, I have no words to speak

It's ALWAYS A RACING thought that seems to unfold,
Scratched ink on parchment paper with a tale formed
By the press of the pen, the quill, the lead of a pencil
Black sores staining the sheet
A process so sublime and yet somewhat obsolete
Scrawled notes scatter the desk that bore wounds of the years sat standing
With rage fueled scars created by scraping of walls and fists pounding in fury
Emotional it is to write the chaos that rambles through the fractured mind
Some say like a tornadoes path of ultimate destruction
Emotional it is to bleed the soul onto the paper and stain the desk that holds a delicate work of art with spilled tears running down the battle wearied wood
Comparable it is, the wooden desk of old, passed down from familial generational holding
For the desk holds memories of aged scribbled notes of love or those of blinding fury and rage, and so it is how the walls could speak
Spill words of the painful ideas that tore the delicate sheets of wallpaper like protective skin
The desk, unknown to a raven but aware of the feather, remains a reminder of written sin

THE GLASS SITS on the table, droplets of condensation clinging to its side
She sits at twenty three watching
Trickle down the cup, the crystal clear droplets connect
Remembering car rides for trips out of town when the rain would glow orange
In the night time street lights that lit up the dark forestside road
The moisture collected on the glass was similar to the rain
That rumbled against the window pane, and she watched
In childish glee as the water raced down
Rooting for the smallest of droplets to win
For she was small, she was not made of strength and courage
Instead she was filled with soft feathery down
Ripping open at every wound when a hand lay upon her
A droplet so small, it never stood a chance
Against the hand of the cruel mans advance
The glass sits on the table

Shadows confine me in a pitch black room
The poison in my veins threatens to become blossoming flowers that spill
from my wrists
Seeking escape, freedom from the agony that wails in sorrow
The soil beneath my feet is tainted by the blood filled seeds of desperation
As in the risk, the flight
The kiss of the sharp knife at night brought me to my knees and my roots,
They have broken free of me and wrapped me in their rough embrace,
Pulling me down, pulling me into the earth
Stolen away from where I once felt the whisper of a smile on my lips
As the shadows continue to loom and consume every speck of light that
flickers in my mind
At least I know my death will bring beauty
In the form of a blood stained rose

CURSES PLACED UPON some letters
Mix and match each tainted symbol
Finding deep memories in the rubble
Soon you will see, soon you will know
That there is so much more than what is shown
When you heard the seven letters that make up
The tar beneath the crumbled bricks,
Standing tall where a soul once lived
Crushed to ashes, crushed to dust
It's rather fun to watch my blood rust

Gentle, tender skin that seemed so fragile
Dampened by tears that streamed down her face and dripped
Onto her stained glass heart blown with such careful hatred
Each silver flash brought the tears of the divine
Flowing scarlet, staining crimson
The fragile skin giving in

It is as I lay in the night with the soft glow of dim lights
Finding myself counting hundreds of times
I shake as I breathe and my ears are receptors
To every creak of the wooden floor board
Or thump of footfalls in the hallway stair
A shuddering pound and painful squeak of old metal
Doors slamming, the walls shake
It burns worse than the silver sound of a wailing kettle
Though now I lay me down to sleep in a place that I may call my keep
Fear remaining unpalatable as it stings against my fire breathing heart
I cannot shake the echoing tune
Finding myself quivering in nightmares of dark shadows
Beneath a painted portrait of your sneering face that you burned into my mind

Blinking eyes of dark cinnamon hue
Gaze through the soft frosted glass sea
That was the window to her soul
Where movement had developed a stagnancy
The wispy heartbeats feeling slow
It was different from before,
Far less laughter where once a hiccuping gasp
Echoing through the glass walled rooms
Made the gentleness
So that each day from yonder years and then to those ahead
That held a heavy bucket of glass slivers to pour like rain
Would not pierce the heart she so carefully maintained

A STRANGER IN a bed lay with a few shards in a bag
Somewhere in town, I didn't know the name
Two streets down from where my best friend rested her head
This stranger, his strange lightning eyes steady as he watched me
Pupils blown wide, though not surprised
The small glass pipe that had started with just a little hit
Grown black from the flame
It was always a wonder how long this life sustaining bowl would last
A few more hits of the glass, life destroying as I felt the blast
Wondering when my burning soul that hungered to feast on the world around me
Chaotic as the ravenous gaze of the man
I wished I could turn to ash beneath the strangers grin

WITHERED HUSK OF who I was
Laying in the gentle breeze
My rotted skin being picked apart again
As the vultures of sorrow and pitiful desperation,
Rest their talons and begin the show
Of tearing my flesh into ribbons
As the scars I have left behind
Were not enough to create a memory in the soil beneath where I lay
The monster that I had dissolved into
Built on misery that had long since bled
Devoid of tears that once ran red as the sorrow struck with a razor blade, swift
My empty shell of a being laying in the gentle breeze
Wishing to whisk away on gentle wind
A long forgotten memory

INTO THE MIRROR my eyes wander across
My skin wearied by war
Stark scattered lines and raised pink welts,
The face reflected foreign, it does not belong
A strange creature, perhaps, surely a fantasy
I have washed myself out to sea and donned the cloak of invisibility
Hiding the solemn grip of heartache
That softly echos in my tear rimmed eyes
My war has changed, my war has shaped
Every gasping breath I have and will ever take
This mirror as it reflects the light
Cannot delight in creating the visualizations
Of what beast filled rage and mourning, desperate cries
Living deep in the cage of my bones, cracked and fragile
Clawing at the shape of my soul
The mirror shows only a hole

Six years and my heart still breaks into thousands of tiny silver pieces
Not the gratitude of gold for that had been her
But silver is a good replacement for
The scarlet dripping where my soul should be resting and staining the bed
With crimson misery, endless tears that come
From this unforgettable travesty
There is no forgiveness for the God who struck down
A lightning eyed beauty bearing now a glowing halo crown
No King can move mountains yet I'd move continents
For the simple five minutes with the tiny, fragile girl
Who left to soon and in her place
Six years later I am still left with
Tiny silver pieces

Shuttled fracture of my soul
Launched into space where the oxygenous waste
Carbon dioxide the main replace
Every breath a shaking gasp
As the plucked memories come rushing past
I have flown to space and settled in the rust
Of the infectious disease of humanity
With the wonder of how interesting it was
Though that was not the easiest to say
Direct volatility was what made her chest
Where lungs clutched the emptiness
With stinging razor claws
It was still a pain that I found less painful
Than the day I lost you

Fundamentals of alchemy define
That something cannot be gained without the loss
Perhaps in the manner of speaking these laws
That guide a treasure map fantasy
It was the loss of your infectious grin
Where soiled tissues of crumpled crimson stain
Were hidden in the back of your mind,
In a window sort of view
Have you ever felt
The reality scam so deep that it echos
In the sliver of bones

How SORROWFUL the words become
When desperation survives
Though sadness of a total heart
That falls into its sorrow
For the frantic pump
The shiver of dear held memories
It's a wonder we don't all escape the lives that we so dread
In pieces of shattered, fractured
Antiquities

IF ONE WERE to go so far and claim
That it is sorrow that washes them from the bay
Where we are taken by the lunging waves
Torn breaths shaken from our inflating gasps
The water how it pulls us so
Into the deep, into the throw
How much like grief the river flows
With tender words and rapids growing

I GASP FOR the air I wish to fill my lungs
Where water of substance, remedied torture
Fills every inhale while I sink deeper under
Crimson signs pool at my feet
Blood that leaks from my alabaster heart
Every beat, pulsating
Silently the water fills the spiderweb
Of veins that have wasted, sentenced to a death so pitiful
By the crushed up medication melody
I gasp for air, but instead I push down on the plunger
Close my eyes, let the water and the crimson stains
Take me under

SULFUR STARS DOTTING shadowed eyes
Every breath where she wishes to be cauterized
Let life wash away from those soul filled skies
Heart beats ever lasting until one of us
Dies as the sky above, sun below
Galaxy signals seem so slow
Desperate gasps pull back
Plungers depressing in scarlet hues
Eyelids close and drift away
Peaceful patterns, what can I say
When just moments pass
Perhaps too late, thoroughfare thoughts
Melting patterns of fractured desperation
How many words can be said in contemplation
Describe a lifelong malady
One, two, twenty more
These yellow marigold pills hold so tight
If there were to ever be any freedom in sight
Syringes piercing skin has a wonder
What world have I become such a monster
Within
Escaping is miles of agonizing leaps away
Lord please help my flickering hope
Crumbling under the weight
Every needlepoint scar
Side-eyed stare, judgemental glare
Some dozen passing years never enjoyed nor hoped for
Far from here, distanced from the smile
Once gracing pink lips turned blue
Never forgetting such sorrowed whispers
Wishing I could crawl back to you

WHY DO BATTERED wounds taste better
Than the drip of love that trickles
In desperate stalactite ridden caves
I have hidden myself in a quiet sort of way
A new home for my heart that bleeds
The thick crimson smear creating floors
Where stalagmites grow and reach
The glistening, sorrowed tears that whisper
A question we all wonder
Why do battered wounds taste better
Than the feeling of the reciprocity of love

In the shadow here I see
Faces staring back at me
The ones that lingered in the past
And those that have yet come to pass
They are faces of my own
Split with smiling scarred fear
You haunted my dreams in the wicked way
Where you had survived to see so many days
Where when you grinned and your teeth turned to ash
I stilled begged and prayed
That I could get you back

HOSTAGE SEEMS a simple word
A battled wearied warrior seems slightly on the contrary
Mayhaps the dark and thunderous nights
Where a werewolf bite seemed to be a kinder peace
Than your foul acid breath and a sneer
Hands running along my skin
Desperate screaming internally, I wished to be free
Of the prison of flesh I had wounded so secretly
For maybe once I had been a hostage to your cruelty
Instead I am now a haunted memory
You may have left me bleeding, alive, by what some
Would claim to be a grace of the divine
No, it was not grace, it was not beauty
It was purely cruelty to leave me alive
With new scars dancing in my eyes
I wished I was a hostage again
Instead, you left a part of me dead
Like a limb grown shadow black
Appendages of sour gangrene
A carcass of who I was
Hostage seems a simple word, just as terror
Created by your ravenous hunger
As you took that which was not yours with such a greedy grasp
When you left me in the stench of your cruelty
I did not survive, I am shattered glass

It had been spoken in gentle words
A broken record echoing few
Tuneless sounds and cracking cues
Mismatched words carried a song
Of hope, of bitterness, of holding on
Tentative and hesitant were those who dared listen
To the wisdom words that came with a lesson
Many had hoped and many did wonder
If this broken record spoke to the sadness
Encasing the heart, the shadows on the mind
Perhaps the bitter leaves of nettle that clung to each breath
As the music pulled tears to their eyes, heaving sobs aching their chest
It is so as the saying goes,
A broken record still plays
Despite that it had seen brighter days
I knew when I heard that record scratch
Against all that I had fought back
I would still continue to play
In spoken gentle words

DARKNESS LURKS WITH my chest
Clutching on to every breath
Some say it is sorrow, some say it is rage
I say it is a payment
For getting away
I may have survived
With battle wearied skin
And a heart that likes to ooze
But still the remnants of the past
Sting with every breath
As if similar to the slice
Of glass, of the secrets that have been written
In the scarlet streaks
This darkness, it cannot be treated
So I say perhaps it is time to wave the white flag

Hovering with a cloak in waiting, as if a gentle mother
Claws that seek to tear my sense of home
Dragging peaceful strokes across my skin
Inviting the bubbles of crimson again
Lurking in the dark shadows, she breathes
Each lightbulb flickering as the lines dance, bending to her will
Darkness is an odd sensation for those aware of the presentation
Knowing there in the shade where the light does not shine
Lives a beast with a curved, wicked grin
Who directs our otherworldly sin

COLDER THAN the arctic snow
Far less a beautiful sight
Yet the sting of icy winds is comparable
To the touch of your hand against my flesh
Where my body is so fragile
As the turmoil and raging rapids of the emotions
Have become branded into me like a cow to the slaughter
It is a pain I know, a shared testimony
Filling those with broken hearts
Tarnished souls
Memories that never grow
As cold as the arctic snow

POISON LEECHES THROUGH my veins
Dark crimson memories in a portrait of my pain
There is nothing more than a few sips of wine
God, what do I do this time?

IMAGINE ME AS if I were the waves so calm
Perhaps an ocean, so devastating in its beauty
A darkness lurks within the deep
Creatures hungered, gnashing teeth
Still you come into my gentle waves
I pull you in, bringing you home
Into disaster, into chaos, into me
With no warning, my calm waters so rare and deceiving
You are nothing but a speck in the sea

OH HOW DIFFERENT
The sorrow strikes
Where clock hands tick
And the soul,
It hurts
For I am desperate
In a way
To open my eyes
To the time long gone away
What must it be like,
To feel so at home
When every heartbeat
Is the echo of bone

Sᴡᴇᴇᴛ ᴄʜɪʟᴅ,
Oh sweet bliss
When your skin was feathered
With a gentleman's kiss
And sorrow came
To spill the blood,
Anew
It's no further question how one
Came so far
From you

CAN I REMEMBER
Can I bypass
The simple words
That sounded so crass
When a man spoke ill
Of every fine distinctive line
For my veins they bled some plentiful
And his hands,
Well,
They were pitiful
Is it simple for me to forget
Or perhaps, I am simply
One story untold
Yet

If I BLED upon this floor
My wrists an opened door
Where crimson spills
My blood, my pain
Would it bring a benefit
To the white tiled stain
Or perhaps a simple wish
Of a blissful survival
That I do not desire
For every time I take this blade
Oh, every wound this silver has made
Perhaps each heartbeat
Of pulsing blood
Brings for me a deeper part
And an escape
In a tragic art

HERE SO PAINFUL do we wait
With wretched wounds that ooze
Blood and pain
The only answer that seems to find
A foothold, a patience
Every flick of the wrist
Where silver blades create
The scattered red lines
There is no bliss
God, I am so sick of this

THICK DO THE LIES that spill from your lips
As if you had learned so much from this
I see the poison,
Dripping
I see the lies,
Coercion
You are no Saint,
You know the rules
But I can't speak out against
For the pain that you have caused
Because there's simply shattered hearts
That couldn't expect the view
Of the pain
Caused by you

SORROW CHILLS the emptiness
Where sinew and bone create
A body, a person, with so much to see
It is a wonder how much of the blood
That pulses through veins and flows like a river
Through the arteries,
Just so blessed
Not seen by others but seen by me
For books can tell
A thousand stories
But the droplets of blood
Upon the white tile
That scattered, discarded tissue
At least the sorrow
Is born anew

Tears, oh how they flow
Droplets that smear
For makeup and sin
May not go hand in hand
But they mask the covered face
Of the broken hearted
Who lives within
And days go by where I am wondering
What must it be like,
To understand the strike
Of stolen tears
Long forgotten hopes
And a single day
Where we feel hope

Bloody dreams of falling teeth
Cracking skulls and monsters beneath
Rivers flow in crimson hues
The children cry, if not for you
Clutch your babe upon your breast
Find yourself a free flowing fire
Nothing can stop the greed, the Devil's cruel desire

Swallowed water yet there is none
Drowning in a sea that no one else can visualize
Flailing limbs and bloodied skin
These waters,
How they suck me in
Through desperate waves of hungry beasts
Not a second will pass when I
Am at peace

YOUR WICKED WAYS and serpent tongue

The way it's trained me

Since I was young

Where these memories lurk,

Poised to strike,

Prepared to hurt

Salt laden tears and heaving, gasping breaths

What is it that is so wrong

So disgraceful, full of shame

That makes me the damaged part of your

Deadly

Poison

Game

I SAT IN WAVES of blood and sin
Where the color of crimson clashed
With the ivory of my skin, where the blood I spilled
Poured down my hand, the gaping wounds
Screaming in the numbness of severed nerves
A heartbeat pounding to the same of the blood pumping from my veins
I remembered all the pain I held within
Forever remembering the hands that touched my complexion
Turned a soft smile into a fallen from grace expression upon my face
I sit in this ocean that crashes against me
Watch as the life of me pours from my soul
Perhaps I am never going to be free
But if I sit in these waves of blood and sin
Does that mean I am a person
Again

I PLANTED SEEDS within the soil
Spread upon it the tears that spilled
From the day you walked away
As while there is no beauty in the pain
Of the slashed scars and severed veins
At least I have found a way
To create something new

I AM a masterpiece
By which I mean I am fragmented
Shattered bones and slaughtered skin
My body is a work of art
If violence at my own hand,
A silver blade and flickering flame,
Created more than just another falling star

DRAGGED INTO the mirrored room
Where screams of echoed pasts
Can't seem to come to pass
Bouncing off the walls and ringing my ears
My head, how it feels so full
Tipping points of shattered hopes
Desperate cries as bones protrude
This skin is my foreword

DECOMPOSING in my veins
Blood that stains the soil
Feeding flowers from my pain
I am so tired as these poppies grow
At least I can say that this dripping crimson
Fed more than just the hunger
To be a part of something greater
So as my blood seeps into the petals
And the wind, she blows them gently
You will hear my voice softly whisper
Forgive me, once again

Pulsing veins with
Glass-like shattered hearts
Cracks that form a story
Blood that pools, sorrowfully
Violent beating, echoing gasps
Keeping alive a body so worn, so tarnished
So tired of the dismal rain
And to the crimson that which spills
Upon white tile, creating a stain
Pulsing veins, there's nothing left
I am bereft

Oh here, how fair flows the river
Its white rapids tempting to pull me
Under
Into the frigid, crushing embrace
While I remember bloodied saving grace
A single tear on the strings
This river will make me whole
Again

Sorrow's blade may bleed
In frantic breaths;
Of ink to page
In screams at night
Echoing sounds of hallowed
Shattered souls that have been cut so feverishly
By both a hand, a blade
That takes sorrow
As its name

BLESSINGS ARE SPOKEN in shattered thoughts
A blind man's love lost like his sight
I wish I could repair these endless segments of scratched, panicked words
That I have bled onto the page
Poured from the wounds of my soul shriven carcass, slivers of dripping scarlet hue
This blind man may be blessed with his plunge into darkness, away from sunlight
And gentle wearied whispers of palatable sound
All I can see are mistakes I have made
While I may not be blind, I cannot be found

It is on rivers of malady
That creates such sinful formality
A graceful walk, a prideful hope
Nailed to a stake, burned at the cross
I am torn from this illusion of future
Lost in tidal waves and pulled together
By dark blue, twisting sutures
This river once a flowing vein
Now a torn and shredded stain
Destined to run dry
Again

Mirrored walls with streaked stains of sinful portrayed
Disasters ways where paint
It bleeds so forgotten, sideways words
Of lies that drop to the ground as if
Wings once flourished became
Clipped sorrow and battle stained
So fruitless failure proves once again
A simple smile
Is nothing gained

I REMEMBER TAINTED blissful kisses
As hands crawled along unblemished skin
Where words escaped and hearts collided
Who have thought love was so
One-sided

WEARY DAYS COME to pass,
I find myself trapped
My thoughts, a raging fire
That not even holy water can devour
For these words that build so viciously
Aligned into sentences of pure sadistic misery
I am left burning into ash
Watching weary days
Come to pass

PENNY FOR your thoughts
Mine aren't worth a sputtered breath
Each empty echo pulling me
I wish so feverishly that my hummingbird heartbeat
Would come to something slower
And my thoughtless malady would end
Just not in travesty

Autumn leaves crumble and echoed laughter sings
Memorized days of sunshine rays
Snow that falls upon the ground,
The crisp sound of memories filtering in again
I miss the days when I had my friends,
The love that once filled my days has drifted far away
And though the days of autumn leaves and snowman games are long behind
I'll never forget the days
When I called you mine

I WISHED I could see a future of light
Yet instead I fear I am going to see
Empty beds, clinking bottles, nothing more than breathless ends
A sorrowful life full of echoed pain
I cannot escape, I cannot relive it again
Please, for one moment, just let me feel free
And then I will return to endless malady

Bones, in aching arms I feel a stranger
Amongst the sinew that binds me
Together
Each rib is more than the building blocks that create my stone hearts cage
These alabaster sorrows hold in place
A delicate teetering race,
Each heartbeat slams into the calcified confinement
With each scream and fluttering thrum, I crumble
While my soul begins to decay
At least my cold, stone-filled heart cannot be washed away

Nameless poems

Are written from the depths

As deep as the ocean floor,

Where the light does not reach

These words crawling out when emotion becomes too real

I feel your absence

Like a missing part of my heart, my soul

You were not nameless,

Though you now remain in the depths of my past

Flustered breaths and crashing hearts
Beating thoughts, a work of art
Gentle memories and foreword screaming
It is fear that keeps me from that step
As I stand at a cliff,
Wondering what it must be like to fall
Into silent sorrow and gentle emptiness

Bloated corpse full of decay
A soul long given into the sin
Of pressing veins and needles in
A rush for just a moment
A delightful fatal component
Ice it was and ice it will be
That leaves me
Another fatality

TIRED EYES can't seem to close
These nightmares circle my mind
I cannot forget those hands that once
So tender, so full of love, so calm
How could they have become so violent and cruel
Turned against me,
Bruising my blood and bone
A reminder that my memories
Will forever be set in stone

ECHOED THOUGHTS that trickle-down
A rain cloud, so to speak
That lingers just a bit too long,
Hiding the sun as it rises
Breaking apart the rays of light
Yes, I am in the dark
What more is there to say
For there is not a single day that passes smooth and free
Where I don't wonder what it must be like
To simply fade away

INTO THE EYES of the sun
Where burning bright sin can be reflected
In rippling water, the dancing rays
Would I sink if I were to swim,
Or burn up in my own reminiscing
As the catastrophic, drastic pain
Lends me a memory
Of when the sun once brought hope
Instead of the days now where I hide from her gaze
Trapped inside the walls that consume
Every sound, every beat
Of my tired, aching
Fallen heart

No ONE UNDERSTOOD what kept us together
Love, it can't be helped even if by a sinner
So we wait until the day we'll say our 'I dos,'
Move to a country or perhaps a bustling city,
And we would start anew
We'll be happier than ever, take one day at a time
At least, we would, if they were still mine.

IF I PAINTED a picture there'd be nothing but pink,
If I wrote you a song it would be nothing but my heart beating to every strum of your chords,
Tracing the wood of your guitar,
Plucking the strings as I felt your heartbeat match mine
We were crazy to fall in love so fast, but isn't that how it happens? Just like that?
There was something about holding you that just felt right
I'll never forget when I lost you
That cold distant night

Exhaustion in the silence
Fog rolling in my carcass of a life
Silent thoughts that bounce,
Echoing memories that I cannot escape
Instead, I'll take this small glass
Fill it full of brass colored sorrow
Chug the liquid and feel the burn,
At least then I could be five steps ahead
Of the sorrowful act that I would one day commit,
A suicide that kept me holding my breath

Dancing with the flames
My skin, sizzling and popping
The blisters charred,
Silent screams held by clenched teeth
Deserved sorrow, echoed chatter
It is the easiest solution
To my own execution

WOULD IT BE so much of a disastrous,
Catastrophic,
World ending,
Collapse of the thought,
If I begged for the God's that we all once believed,
To give me just one day of softness,
Where kindness reigns
Instead of this endless, silent regime

CASTAWAY IN A river of crimson,
This bathtub an ocean,
This spilling blood is no longer an illusion
I tempt fate, I tempt the Gods
I prove to myself,
In such a strange manner,
That I am capable of taunting those above me
I guess you could say, in so few words
I'm not like my mother
I'm more of a rebel
Finding it a miracle I survived past
The severed momentary breath

What was I saying,
Oh, I just cannot remember
But this blood, this memory of silver gleam
At least I know I have done what is best
In what I can only see as a dream

Scarlet sin,

Cold weather leaving puffs of clouds' breath,

I watch as this snow,

So white and so pure

Becomes a reminder of the humanity

What lurks within my smothering, choking theft

Of a life I was meant to have,

And instead am left buried in an avalanche

Chaotic emotions doing a sort of mediocre dance

Trying not to be left, trying not to be right

Afraid, perhaps watching the pulsating sight

As this once gentle poetry,

Become a chaotic rendition of

Oh, I don't know

It's just a simple game

THERE'S SOMETHING COLD about the way I live my life. Cold like the
numbness that comes during the first winter days,
Where the snow falls soft, the sky a gentle gray hue
And the wind blows harsh ice, coating the roads, creating danger
I must say, as the fear pulses from bloodied wounds,
Life is boring, an endless stretch of personal eternity until the sweet re-
lease that can only be found with death
Something that comes to take the breathing people, sometimes in their
slumber, sometimes as they drive their cars,
I seek games and you'd be surprised,
I am the toy,
The razor blade is simply winters cold kiss
While the blood spills from my wrist

I have an obsession
It starts with a breath,
A single escape,
The desperation of chosen theft,
Stolen life and empty words,
Death brings the only solitary silence,
It is what I seek so patient
Within my waking hours
For while I slumber, drifting into imaginary worlds
It ends with a blast, some crimson spurts,
A single kiss

Some imagine death to be a peaceful blackness,
Others a place of peaceful serenity
Finality of thought, no pain nor joy
That is yet still what I fear,
Despite this obsession that consumes my waking pacing thought
I fear that I will miss great joys, which is solely a given
Yet I do not see life bringing me anything but inescapable boredom
Desperate echoes that pain my chest and cause my head to throb with
every sound that rings around me
I live in a trapped eternity,
I can't wait for the sweet release of finality

I am a fool with no decoration,
A girl who deserves no admiration
I am loved, I have lost
I am once changed by so much that has cost the friendships that once

Held together by fragile twine
Kept my heart beating, my soul alive
I'll never forget the day she walked through the door
Never to turn again,
Her blue eyes never to see me,
Forevermore

I SCRIBBLE ON paper and wonder
Do these words have meaning
Or am I a wannabe
Where nothing I write is chaotic enough
Not poetic, all in vain
Yet I find such peace in the spread of ink
The paper scarred, just as my skin
Splits and sends the words flowing
I scribble on paper,
Because it's better than carving
Into my flesh
Though some would say,
And this is just a guess
There is nothing more that I do best

I DON'T KNOW the beginning or the end of my story
Yet none of us do
Where our eyes may close in one split second
Or perhaps we'll live 'til gray and old
We don't know what the middle holds
My beginning, it is full of holes
I am scared that in the middle there will be nothing
Save for more chaotic destruction,
Bloodstained clothes and swallowed pills
I wish I were much easier to kill

I AM a demon in my own body,

A poison to my soul

Do I want to turn away,

See the light of days to come

Or if I want to set this course, hit the wall head-on?

I no longer know whether I want to live or die

I know more of what confused me and less of what I once understood

Yes, I am a stranger in my body

And perhaps that is all that is mine

Shadows cast,
The dripping blood
A single blade,
A tiled floor, porcelain tub
One single breath escapes
Before it all
Became too late

THE WORDS, the mumbled chaos
Taking sounds that morph,
Words that echo and songs of force
It echoes in my head,
It rings as it fills me with dread
Please, oh great Gods above
Turn my memories away,
Or drown me in a blood-filled bathtub
As I cannot seem to escape
Each flash and shimmer of a time long ago
Changing the monologue,
Dancing around what once may have been
A truth devoured
By all of my sin

THEY'RE MAKING SOUNDS
Do you hear them?
What do you mean that they aren't real?
See the flash, but when I check it
No, I know I saw it
Nothing.
Oh, how they taunt me
How the chanting words envelop me
Please these sounds, these grating chimes
Perhaps I will pray
To an old divine
For silence and peace, for just one breath
That isn't caught in my chest
And as I am stolen into the echoing chambers of fluctuating screams
They're making sounds,
I will forever wonder
If this is all a dream

I CANNOT LISTEN to birdsong anymore
Where once I heard the gentle chatter
Of winged beings reminding me
What it felt to feel the cold winter air
These monsters in my head
They made it out of thin air, the sound
where I sat in my room
A silent nothing
The sound of my own existence, my ragged breath
They were inside and outside of my head
Filling me full of horror and dread
And they made the sweet sounds of birds passing by
Burrow deep into my skull, and now I wish
That I could kiss the wings of time
And soar silently
Into my own demise

Birdsong has become but an echoing scream of violent pain
Once heard at sunrise with a smile plastered to my face
Listening to the sound of nature is more comfortable than any embrace
I lay in wake in the early morn and feel as if the sound is a thorn
Grating screams and crows of rage
Dig into my scribbled journal page
For once my skull had echoed the song
Of a bird that bellowed a horrific tune of desperation and lay before me
awaiting eternal damnation
I once loved the beautiful echo of a birdsong
And now I sit with spilled ink
Realizing no, it is not the song that grates against my eardrums
Nor the soft feathers that float so careful in the wind
It is the privilege of their freedom
Something I have not seen nor felt
As the bars around me encase me
And I am left alone in my all-consuming insanity

I HAVE NO more words to speak

No fancy lies of twisted divine intervention

Unless one should count the deep screams yelling into an abyss that taunts me

With the depth I'd fall, my wings no longer catching the air that whips against my skin

Courage is what it would take to take that step

Final freedom and the fearful excitement burns in my crimson-stained chest

Abysmally drained, exhaustion keeping the actions at bay despite the chanting words

It lingers in my poisoned mind, that endless thought

Unanswered prose of burning crows as they scream into the night

The thoughts as they echo and strike fearful horror

Dare I venture to crawl from this bed in which I lay

Where the sheets provide a world of peace

A gentle silence, a poetic lease as it keeps me contained in the shadows of my cloaked bedroom

Or shall I never have to move again, with my final breath choking on bloodstained lines of poetry that never leave my fragile mind

Still, I have no words to speak

WASTED FOOD sits on a plate
Plastic utensils lay in wait
A slice of bacon, a slice of toast
It feels as massive as a Sunday roast
These simple calories feel empty to me
Where I wish I did not need to seek
The fuel to keep my body
Oh, I am so weak

I HAVEN'T been able to eat anything
Perhaps the droplets of cream in my coffee
Will sustain this life of broken dreams
It's 6:00 pm and the idea of more
Than just a teardrop spilled
I'm sore
I guess it's just another day gone by

ONCE I THOUGHT of you and felt this feeling
Where my heart soared
As if the clouds had become my thread
That kept me tied to this world
You were so beloved
I wonder, what made it end?

CATASTROPHIC pain can only cause
Confusion and cataclysmic thoughts
My love for you, it sat so strange
So I took that little needle
Plunging poison in my veins

WATCH the painters brush
Strike a pose as your lips turn blue
This silver blade, it hits the cue
Of slaughtered veins counting one to two
My death will be so crimson-stained as white tiles change
My brush a metal razor blade, each wound upon my canvas, fate was changed
Yet still, I yearn for thrice more works, perhaps this artistry beholds a curse

It was heartbreaking to say goodbye to you
But it was so much harder
Saying farewell to the version of myself
That once loved you

PEACE, FREEDOM, the soft wind blowing against my skin
The warmth of the sun beating down upon me
The laughter of my friends creates a calm I have never before known
I have lived and loved; lost and been found
But now I am once again the person I so dreamed to be
Oh, I can't even lie in my poetry

I HAD GROWN from a life of pain, of struggles and illness that left rivers of
blood in my wake
Yet I was and have always been a survivor
With the dark circles under my eyes
A few prayers whispered, some gentle cries
I can become so much more, and I will one day

IN FRONT OF you, I stand
With silent words and tear-filled eyes
I know the truth, and so do you
Perhaps there's a way we can move on
But I will never forgive you

Castaway beliefs that fill the starlit sky
Songs of faded memories that whisk away sincerity
Alone beats the echo of my heart
My love as distant as the stars
Spaced apart

DEPRESSION sinking in my chest
A God I believed in,
He has since left
I am alone with this heart filled with broken sorrow
I do not wish to see tomorrow

I AM ALONE, I am free
Maybe not to be me
For the person I am is sad and lost
I wish I could cross the path to freedom
Where I smile, feel peace
Instead, I am a wasted heart
And bleeding wounds,
My best art

In my heartless echoed sorrows
Screaming yet there is no echo
To the ground, I scrape my knees
As I fall and feel this
Begging, desperation
Wishing for the beauty of
A butterfly wings freedom
If I could truly be me

I WONDER what the stars would say
Their only friend, the moon,
The drifting decay of travelled time
Comets passing by, broken into pieces
I wish in ways that I were a comet
Forever alone, forever passing by
Or a star in collapse
Anything would be better
Than this relapse

DARK SORROW sucks the stream of blood
My veins poisoned by tarnished
Dirty and decaying
Emotions
That feel so strong and so inescapable
Does it ever get better?

SCATTERED LAUGHTER like tooth decay
An outcast sworn on day to day
I'd rather be sore, my nerves exposed
Than live another lonely year
Who am I kidding,
It is all that I know

In the darkness, awake I lie
Alone for yet another day
Like the rolling of a die
It is not by choice, it is by sorrow
I know that tomorrow will bring no change
Perhaps these low scoring dice can be rearranged
For creatures of habit tend not to change
And I trapped within confines
Of the plunged into darkness,
Monstrous cage

GENTLE does the river flow
Like chaos in the winter snow
A crimson stain, a slit of bliss
It is no tenderness that lead to this
For gentle may the river flow
It is no softness when my heartbeat slows

ECHOING SORROW through my heart
Where once a dance, a work of art
I am alone, I am lost at sea
Somewhere I was lost to melancholy
In this battle, in this war
I fester like an open sore
And loneliness it eats away
Triggering sensations of crippling decay

I WONDER what it must feel
Perhaps a ballad so surreal
To melt into the warm embrace
A gentle touch, no warning brace
Love is long been a mystery
And I
A walking travesty

ONCE IT WAS NOT lost upon me
A shattered soul so whisked away
I knew the touch of tender care
So briefly yes but it was there
Yet nowadays I sink into
A large sprawling bed meant for two
Where I rest my head from dusk till dawn
Wondering where it is I have
Gone wrong

LONELINESS SO DULL and lacking hue
This world of colour now so blue
Perhaps a gray ocean but even still
I wade through the waters,
I drink the swill
I feel the waves that crash into
My desolate beaches with no footsteps true
Knowing no day will be the same
No longer smiling, showing only pain
The way I did before
Where once soft caresses and gentleness flew
Now I am missing when I was beside
You

WEAKNESS in my petal soft skin
Torn with ease, a view of within
Veins snake and crawl along my wrists
Yearning for the ending, oh such sweet bliss
Divine the intervention when my wilted soul
Will be free of this flower confined,
In rooted wrong soil,
My stem and leaves grow cold

I am weaponized in my own chaos
A dagger wielded from shattered glass mirrors
Where fists of rage now crumbled and cracked
With blood that seeps through the pressed fingers
These wounds I create that bleed oh so lovely
Are perhaps something worse than the scars
I wish I could see myself somewhere far
From this chaotic view
Where my dangerous sight and endless pain
Continuously makes
A scarlet debut

PLEASE forgive me for
These bundled vague mistakes
I did not care, I did not see
Who knew it'd cause a travesty
I could use some tape to fix
These split scars that gape
With emotions overflowing
Perhaps a bit of glue
To keep me together
A little while longer
While I dream of tearing myself
In two

I AM STARING into the blue
An ocean deep bloodied sinew
Yet this blue appears to be
A crimson dark malady
For every heartbeat comes a pulse
And every pulse a rivered dose
Pumping my freedom, pumping my life
From within me
To the once pink pyjamas that I sit
Remembering nothing of what it was
That made me feel so sick

It was desperation
It was home
How she felt, so less alone
When clinking cutlery no longer seemed
A violent household memory
Shattered screens and calamity scenes,
It's appears so contrary
To movie magic gleam reminders
Where this desperation is only met
With confusion, a lost soul
Taking her down under

I HAD LOVED this girl of mine,
She lived in peaceful passing time
Forever stuck a young sixteen
I'd never forget the day, that dream
Better spoken as a nightmare scene
When the words were spoken into the air
I learned the reality of
"Life's not fair"

I LOVED the way the ocean moved
The deep and patient moving blues
The bubbling waves, the frothing hues
But never could I love anything more
Than you

THESE DELICATE SCARS on paper thin skin
Are fragile and made of
A sin from within
They litter my flesh, yard upon yard
Pink streaks, purple catching
A story of catastrophe and far
Far away pains and desperate screaming cries
Of a life once lived, when clocks ticked with dreams of one's demise
Unforgotten be these moments of terror
Of shame, no redemption
Never forgotten, the white tile floors
These delicate scars,
Of a time once so poor

I FELT YOU in the cold winter air
The bite against my cheek as the wind
So calmly whispered in my ear
Reminding me of things so dear
Like when my dog would bury himself
In snow covered grass and warm blankets
I felt you in the memories
When I walked down a hill and began to slide
Remembering when we would hide
In ice forts made precariously
Giggling as the candles flickered and the ice
How to glistened, it was so nice
I feel you in the days so fair
I'll always wish that you
Were here

Paint smeared on walls in shame
Crimson coloured, not hard to name
It is not pain used in creation
Droplets formed from desperation
This love, it hurts so deep
I've lost so many hours of sleep
And so I paint with a canvas of skin
And tear apart the soul within

Crashing waves of ocean delight
Mountain ranges viewed in distant sight
Birds on wings that tilt and curve
The freedom found, the freedom earned
I wish I could feel the wind beneath
The wings that give my heart its beat
Yet I stare at the world around me and feel
The sway of terror, an even keel
I have not forgotten the desperate views
Of smeared bloodstains and camera rooms
While I may not fly in freedom with the wind
I may not spread my wings held within
I instead sing my own holy tune
Free from distant memories that once
Filled me with nothing but fright

I SOUGHT out a love anew
Yet yearned for something out of the blue
I'd never loved so deep and true
My heart closed off to all but few
Alone I walk these empty rooms
Drag my fingers in trails along
Blank walls where memories of gloom
All different, all a mediocre sing-song
Are the only ones that play in repetition
For I am lost to trepidation
Alone in my annihilation
I sought out love, I sought it true
But nothing can replace you

So WEARY each day
A memory both smeared and painted
Horrified fright, delicate strokes as we pray
Watching in views so tainted
And the way a hand stretches forward
We see it in such a framed fabrication
The sin that comes in search of reward
Acted with ease, such a terrified revelation
These weary eyes struggle to stay open
Perhaps I am the one who is broken

I DO NOT KNOW what it is to love
For those I once held in my heart
Are distant and so many years apart
And the love I've felt was never not strange
A foreign emotion I've locked in a cage
It lurks in parchment of turned paper page
In passed whispers along the giggles and waves
It is found in the touch of a hand on one's cheek
And I perhaps am just simply
Just far too weak

YARDS OF FLESH that feel so foreign
Cling to my bones, the sinew tearing
Muscles wasted, every sensation disorienting
I trace a finger on my palm, contact
It stings like the bite of a snake
Injecting venom, reminding me of fate
Perhaps fake I feel, perhaps strange I am
My skin it feels so weathered
My foreign flesh corrugated
I trace a finger on my palm
Reminded this prison is not
My home

Exhausted eyes so sullen faced
Weighed down by years of formed disgrace
These blinking blues cannot seem to find
Nor see a day we seek,
Sublime
We tumble in the dark sky anew
Born under the sun, born under the moon
Rest is such a scarcity
For we live in cities of tragedy
And though we lay our heads to rest
Our hearts pace on inside our chest
Exhausted eyes that yearn to close
We cannot find our long forgotten
Home

THERE'S AN ANGER that tends to flow through me
It feels foreign yet homely
Many cannot forgive and I simply cannot forget
I refuse to release these memories, to see the past freed from me
Hard desperation and angered words have lingered in my heart
I worked for this rage
And I will work to one day remember
I am no longer trapped in a cage

Manufactured by Amazon.ca
Bolton, ON